PEOPLE WHO HELP KEEP ME HEALTHY

By JANET PREUS

Illustrated by CHARLOTTE COOKE & DAN CRISP

CANTATA LEARNING

MANKATO, MINNESOTA

WWW.CANTATALEARNING.COM

CANTATA LEARNING

MANKATO, MINNESOTA

Published by Cantata Learning
1710 Roe Crest Drive
North Mankato, MN 56003
www.cantatalearning.com

Library of Congress Control Number: 2014957004
978-1-63290-271-9 (hardcover/CD)
978-1-63290-423-2 (paperback/CD)
978-1-63290-465-2 (paperback)

People Who Help Keep Me Healthy by Janet Preus
Illustrated by Charlotte Cooke

Book design, Tim Palin Creative
Editorial direction, Flat Sole Studio
Executive musical production and direction, Elizabeth Draper
Music arranged and produced by Steven C Music

Printed in the United States of America.

VISIT
WWW.CANTATALEARNING.COM/ACCESS-OUR-MUSIC
TO SING ALONG TO THE SONG

It's no fun being sick, and having a **toothache** hurts. It's a good thing that there are people who can help you feel better. Are you ready to meet the people who help you stay healthy?

Now turn the page, and sing along.

Doctors and dentists,

nurses, hygienists

help me be healthy!

I didn't eat my breakfast. I really don't feel good.

Mom takes me to the **clinic**. I was pretty sure she would.

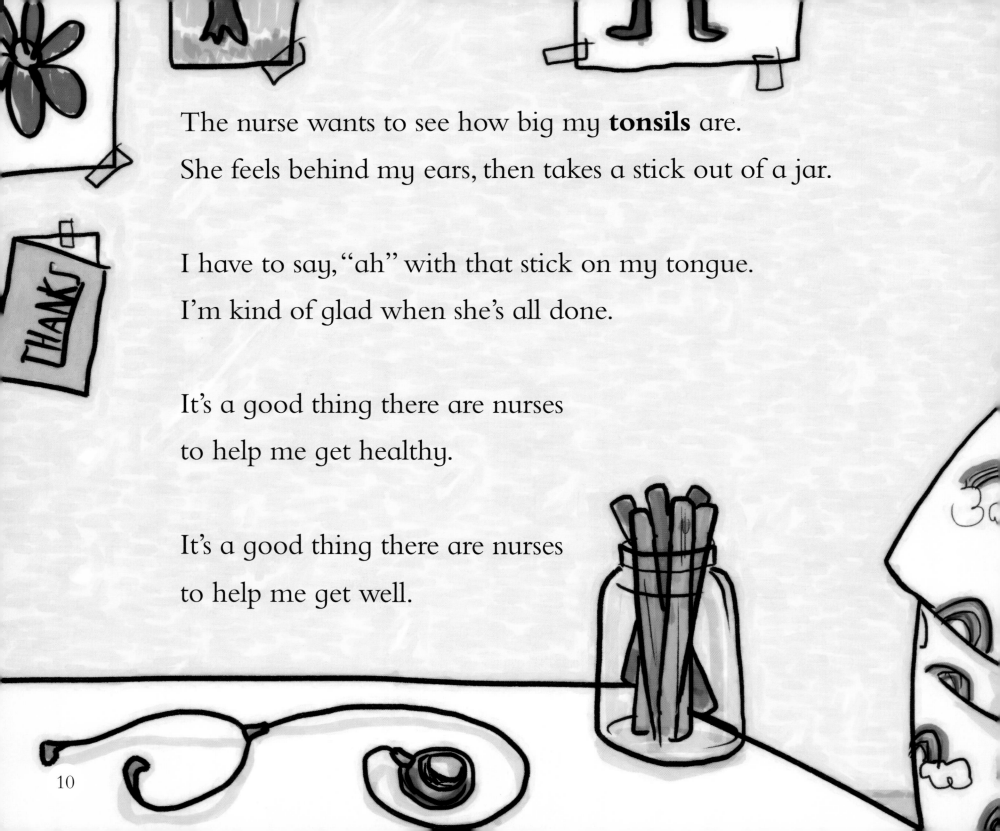

The nurse wants to see how big my **tonsils** are.
She feels behind my ears, then takes a stick out of a jar.

I have to say, "ah" with that stick on my tongue.
I'm kind of glad when she's all done.

It's a good thing there are nurses
to help me get healthy.

It's a good thing there are nurses
to help me get well.

The doctor knows why I'm sick and why I'm moving slow.
She tells me, "Take your **medicine**," then back to bed I go.

It's a good thing
there are doctors
to help me get healthy.

It's a good thing
there are doctors
to help me get well.

You should see the dentist, especially when you're small.

I go twice a year, in the spring and in the fall.

The **hygienist** checks my gums and teeth. I think it's kind of fun.

I get a brand new toothbrush when the cleaning's done.

It's a good thing there are hygienists
to help me stay healthy.

It's a good thing there are hygienists
to help me stay well.

I was a little worried when the dentist saw my tooth.

"Oh, my!" she said. "How can you eat? It's so very loose."

Then suddenly my baby tooth was sitting on a tray.

"Here's your tooth," she said, and all my worries went away.

It happened so fast. I can't even tell you how.

But I feel much better, and I like my smile now!

It's a good thing there are dentists
to help me stay healthy.

It's a good thing there are dentists
to help me stay well.

19

It's a good thing there are people
to help me stay healthy.

It's a good thing there are people
to help me stay well.

I'm happy, healthy, well.
Thank you doctors and dentists,
nurses, hygienists
for helping me be healthy!

SONG LYRICS
People Who Help Keep Me Healthy

Doctors and dentists,
nurses, hygienists
help me be healthy!

I didn't eat my breakfast. I really don't feel good.
Mom takes me to the clinic. I was pretty sure she would.

The nurse wants to see how big my tonsils are.
She feels behind my ears, then takes a stick out of a jar.

I have to say, "ah" with that stick on my tongue.
I'm kind of glad when she's all done.

It's a good thing there are nurses
to help me get healthy.
It's a good thing there are nurses
to help me get well.

The doctor knows why I'm sick and why I'm moving slow.
She tells me, "Take your medicine," then back to bed I go.

It's a good thing
there are doctors
to help me get healthy.

It's a good thing
there are doctors
to help me get well.

You should see the dentist, especially when you're small.
I go twice a year, in the spring and in the fall.

The hygienist checks my gums and teeth. I think it's kind of
    fun.
I get a brand new toothbrush when the cleaning's done.

It's a good thing there are hygienists
to help me stay healthy.

It's a good thing there are hygienists
to help me stay well.

I was a little worried when the dentist saw my tooth.
"Oh, my!" she said. "How can you eat? It's so very loose."

Then suddenly my baby tooth was sitting on a tray.
"Here's your tooth," she said, and all my worries went
    away.

It happened so fast. I can't even tell you how.
But I feel much better, and I like my smile now!

It's a good thing there are dentists
to help me stay healthy.

It's a good thing there are dentists
to help me stay well.

It's a good thing there are people
to help me stay healthy.

It's a good thing there are people
to help me stay well.

I'm happy, healthy, well.
Thank you doctors and dentists,
nurses, hygienists
for helping me be healthy!

People Who Help Keep Me Healthy

Rock
Steven C Music

Pre Chorus
The doctor knows why I'm sick
and why I'm moving slow.
She tells me, "Take your medicine,"
then back to bed I go.

Chorus
It's a good thing there are doctors
to help me get healthy.
It's a good thing there are doctors
to help me get well.

Verse 2
You should see the dentist,
especially when you're small.
I go twice a year,
in the spring and in the fall.

The hygienist checks my gums and teeth.
I think it's kind of fun.
I get a brand new toothbrush
when the cleaning's done.

Chorus
It's a good thing there are hygienists
to help me stay healthy.
It's a good thing there are hygienists
to help me stay well.

Pre Chorus
I was a little worried
when the dentist saw my tooth.
"Oh, my!" she said. "How can you eat?
It's so very loose."

Then suddenly my baby tooth
was sitting on a tray.
"Here's your tooth," she said,
and all my worries went away.

It happened so fast.
I can't even tell you how.
But I feel much better,
and I like my smile now!

Chorus
It's a good thing there are dentists
to help me stay healthy.
It's a good thing there are dentists
to help me stay well.

It's a good thing there are people
to help me stay healthy.
It's a good thing there are people
to help me stay well.

I'm happy, healthy, well.

GLOSSARY

clinic—a place where people go to receive medical care; some doctors have offices in clinics

hygienist—a person who is trained to help a dentist; hygienists clean teeth and take x-rays.

medicine—a substance used for treating an illness

tonsils—flaps of soft tissue that lie on each side of the throat

toothache—pain in or near a tooth

GUIDED READING ACTIVITIES

1. Who are the helpers in this book? What jobs do they do?

2. What can you do to keep yourself healthy?

3. Are there other people who can help you stay healthy?

TO LEARN MORE

Jeffries, Joyce. *Meet the Nurse*. New York: Gareth Stevens Publishing, 2013.

Murray, Aaron R. *Dentists Help Us*. Berkeley Heights, NJ: Enslow Elementary, 2013.

Ready, Dee. *Doctors Help*. North Mankato, MN: Capstone Press, 2013.

Weber, Rebecca. *Healthy Habits*. Mankato, MN: Capstone Press, 2011.